SLED DOGS

by Lori Haskins

Consultant: Wilma Melville, Founder
National Disaster Search Dog Foundation

BEARPORT
PUBLISHING

New York, New York

Special thanks to Wilma Melville who founded the:
National Disaster Search Dog Foundation
206 N. Signal Street, Suite R
Ojai, CA 93023
(888) 4K9-HERO
www.SearchDogFoundation.org

The Search Dog Foundation is a not-for-profit organization that rescues dogs, gives them professional training, and partners them with firefighters to find people buried alive in disasters. They produce the most highly trained search dogs in the nation.

Original design and production by Dawn Beard Creative and Octavo Design and Production, Inc.

Credits

Cover, Front (left), Michel Mory / iStockphoto.com, (top right), Layne Kennedy / CORBIS, (center right), AP / Wide World Photos, (bottom right), Mike Slack / www.team-and-trail.com; Back (top), Layne Kennedy / CORBIS, (center), AP / Wide World Photos, (bottom), Mike Slack / www.team-and-trail.com; Title page, Michel Mory / iStockphoto.com; Page 3, AP / Wide World Photos; 4–5, 6–7, © 2005 Carrie McLain Museum / AlaskaStock.com; 7, Lee Snider / Photo Images / CORBIS; 8-9, © 2005 Anchorage Museum of History and Art / AlaskaStock.com; 9, Lulu Fairbanks Collection, Accession # 68-69-1633, Alaska and Polar Regions Dept., Elmer E. Rasmuson Library, University of Alaska, Fairbanks; 10, AP / Wide World Photos; 11, Mike Slack / www.team-and-trail.com; 12, Jeff Schultz / AlaskaStock.com; 12–13, Paul Souders / Worldfoto; 14-15, Layne Kennedy/ CORBIS; 15, Buddy Mays/CORBIS; 16–17, AP / Wide World Photos; 17, Mike Slack / www.team-and-trail.com; 18-19(both), Jeff Schultz / AlaskaStock.com; 20-21(both), Jeff Schultz / AlaskaStock.com; 22, Danny Lehman/CORBIS; 23, 24–25(both), Jeff Schultz / AlaskaStock.com; 26–27 Paul Souders / Worldfoto; 27, Brittany Colbath; 29(tl), Robert Dowling/CORBIS; 29(tr), Chad Case / Accent Alaska; 29(bl), Prenzel Photo / Animals Animals / Earth Scenes; 29(br), Yann Arthus-Bertrand/CORBIS.

Library of Congress Cataloging-in-Publication Data

Haskins, Lori.
  Sled dogs / by Lori Haskins.
    p. cm.—(Dog heroes)
  Includes bibliographical references and index.
  ISBN 1-59716-171-3 (lib. bdg.)—ISBN 1-59716-197-7 (pbk.)
  1. Sled Dogs—Juvenile literature. I. Title. II. Series.

  SF428.7.H37 2006
  636.73—dc22

                    2005026077

For more information, write to Bearport Publishing Company, Inc., 101 Fifth Avenue, Suite 6R, New York, New York 10003. Printed in the United States of America.

3 4 5 6 7 8 9 10

Table of Contents

Only One Hope   4

A Race Against Time   6

Everyday Heroes   8

Go, Dog, Go   10

No Ordinary Mutt   12

Work and Play   14

Best of the Best   16

Honoring Heroes   18

Enough Is Enough   20

Losing a Leader   22

The Comeback   24

More Than a Sport   26

Just the Facts   28

Common Breeds:
    Sled Dogs   29

Glossary   30

Bibliography   31

Read More   31

Learn More Online   31

Index   32

About the Author   32

Only One Hope

The people of Nome, Alaska, were in trouble. It was January 1925, and a deadly disease had broken out in their town. To treat it, they needed medicine from a hospital in Anchorage, 700 miles (1,127 km) across the snowy **wilderness**.

A sled dog driver is called a musher. The name comes from the French word *marcher*, which means "to walk."

A sled dog team in Nome, Alaska

How could they get the medicine quickly? No roads or train tracks led to Nome. Airplanes couldn't fly there safely in winter weather. Even ships couldn't get through. The sea was frozen! There was only one hope—sled dogs.

Twenty mushers offered to take turns carrying the medicine to Nome. The trip usually took a month. Now, it needed to be done in just a week.

A Race Against Time

Day and night, the sled dogs ran. As the medicine passed from team to team, the weather grew worse.

Fierce wind flung the sleds around like toys. It was so cold, some of the dogs' lungs began to freeze. Then a **blizzard** struck!

Balto (dog in front)
with his sled team

Around the nation, Americans followed the **desperate** race in the newspapers. People worried that the medicine wouldn't make it in time. However, they hadn't heard of a dog named Balto!

Balto and his team ran the last 50 miles (80 km), fighting the storm the whole way. Six days after the trip began, they reached Nome with the medicine. The town was saved!

A statue of Balto in Central Park in New York City

The trip was set up like a relay race. Leonhard Seppala's team, led by a dog named Togo, ran the longest distance—over 250 miles (402 km)!

Everyday Heroes

The rescue in 1925 made Alaska's sled dogs famous. Long before then, however, dogs had been helping humans **survive**.

At least 1,500 years ago, Eskimos **hitched** dogs to sleds. Dogsleds became their first transportation on land.

A sled team in front of the post office in Nome

Later, when the Gold Rush hit Alaska, miners used dogs to carry supplies and gold. Then towns sprang up, and dog teams delivered mail to the settlers. Until 1963, some towns *still* got their mail by sled dogs.

Times were changing, though. Airplanes were built that could fly in cold climates. Snowmobiles were invented. Soon sled dogs were not needed for everyday chores. Luckily they had a more exciting job—racing.

A sign found at the Nome Post Office

During the Gold Rush, Nome had more dogs than people.

Go, Dog, Go

People have been racing sled dogs for over a century. Racing began as a way to pass the winter in **remote** places. Today, it's an international sport. There are races in at least ten U.S. states and a dozen foreign countries.

The World Championship Sled Dog Derby takes place every year in Laconia, New Hampshire.

Twelve-year-old Brittany Colbath lives in New Hampshire. She and her sister, Rachael, who is ten years old, both race sled dogs. "The first time, I was a little scared," admits Brittany. "But after the first mile, it was really fun!"

The girls each have their own dog team. Like most mushers, they drive Alaskan huskies, the top dogs in the racing world.

Some dogsled races are only three miles (5 km) long, while others stretch over 1,000 miles (1,609 km).

Brittany drives a sled dog team. Some teams have 20 or more dogs, depending on the type of race.

No Ordinary Mutt

Alaskan huskies are not **purebred** animals. They are a mix of many kinds of dogs. They have tough, padded feet and thick, warm coats.

These hard-working "mutts" are fast. A team of sled dogs can **sprint** up to 30 miles per hour (48 kph). They're powerful, too. Pound for pound, sled dogs are stronger than horses.

Ramy Brooks

Alaskan huskies are often part Siberian husky, Alaskan malamute, and hound.

Since they are a mixed breed, Alaskan huskies can be all different colors and sizes.

It's not just their bodies that make Alaskan huskies great racers. They love to run, and they're born with an **instinct** to pull.

"Getting them to go is easy," says musher Ramy Brooks. "Getting them to *stop* is the hard part!"

Work and Play

Even though Alaskan huskies are born pullers, they have a lot to learn before they can race. Their training starts simply. Mushers play with the puppies to get them used to people. They teach them to obey **commands**.

When the pups are about one year old, they are hitched to a sled with older dogs to learn teamwork. If a dog can't get along with others, he won't make a good racer.

Finally, at around age two, the dogs start pulling with the team. They go on longer and longer trails to build up strength. In a year, a team might run 3,000 miles (4,828 km)!

When there's no snow, some teams practice by pulling wooden sleds.

Mushers use voice commands to guide the dogs. For example, *Gee* means "turn right," and *Haw* means "turn left."

Best of the Best

During training, a few dogs stand out as smarter and braver than the rest. These dogs become lead dogs. They run at the front of the team and set the **pace** for the other dogs. They also help the musher find and follow the trail, especially in stormy weather.

WELLS FARGO

50

IDITAROD

MUSH WITH P.R.

Sled dog drivers have a deep **bond** with their lead dogs. It's not unusual to hear a musher say, "She's my best friend" or "He's like a brother to me." Once a musher has built a team and found a special dog to lead it, it's time to race.

Some teams have two lead dogs. This is called a double lead.

Robert Sorlie with his two lead dogs—Socks and Blue.

Honoring Heroes

The Iditarod is the longest, toughest, and most famous sled dog race in the world. It honors the heroes who saved Nome in 1925.

The 1,100-mile (1,770-km) trail runs from Anchorage to Nome. Teams cross a wide **tundra**, a steep mountain range, an icy river, and a stretch of frozen sea. The temperature is often far below zero.

Susan Butcher, four-time Iditarod champion, crossing a frozen lake. Women have competed in every Iditarod since 1974.

In these **conditions**, mushers must take special care of their dogs. They feed them several times a day. They put booties on their feet and give them plenty of rest. The dogs' health is more important than anything else— even winning the race.

Even though the booties protect the dogs' feet, some dogs take them off every chance they get!

A meal for the dogs might include moose meat, raw fish, or turkey skin. Mushers sometimes snack on Eskimo ice cream, a mix of reindeer fat, seal oil, and berries.

Enough Is Enough

Despite the special care mushers take, dogs can still get hurt. A dog might cut her foot on the ice, or stumble and pull a muscle. **Frostbite** is a danger for both the dogs and their drivers.

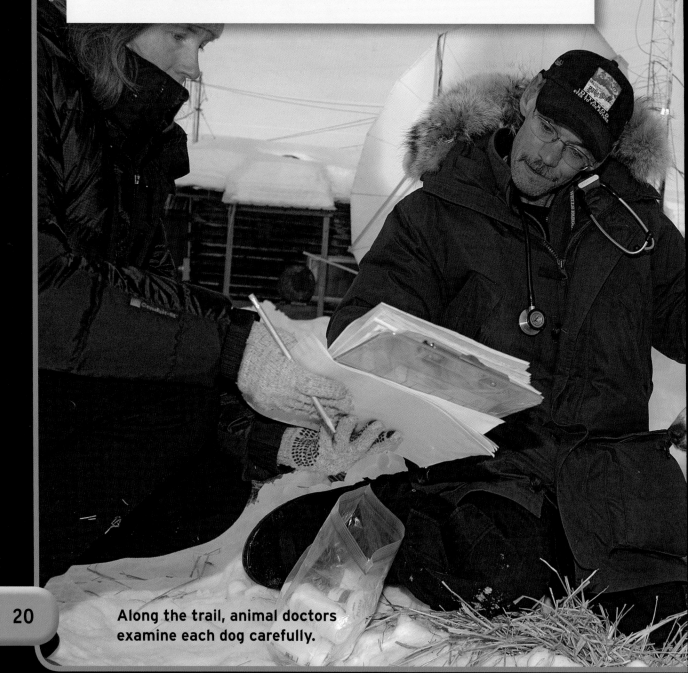

Along the trail, animal doctors examine each dog carefully.

Sometimes dogs get sick or just plain worn out. A musher can tell when a dog has had enough. He may stop eating or being playful. When this happens, the musher has to make a tough decision: should he "drop" the dog from the race?

Dropped dogs are put on planes and flown out of the wilderness. Meanwhile, the rest of the team carries on.

Some dropped dogs are taken to an airplane.

Before the race, each dog has a tiny computer chip placed under his or her skin. The chip lets people keep track of the dogs by computer.

Losing a Leader

In 1998, one of Ramy Brooks's dogs got hurt before the Iditarod even began. It wasn't just any dog—it was his *lead* dog.

With three weeks to go, Pretty Boy stepped in a hole and **injured** his leg. Ramy's heart sank.

The hole Pretty Boy stepped in was left by a moose crossing the trail. Moose holes are a common cause of injury for the dogs.

"Pretty Boy had real drive, and he got the other dogs going, too," said Ramy. "We always ran a good three miles per hour (5 kph) faster with him up front."

Ramy had no choice but to put another dog in the lead. He ended the race in 17th place. It was a good finish, but he had hoped to do better.

Ramy Brooks and his team competing in the 1998 Iditarod.

There is no limit to the number of teams in the Iditarod. Usually around 65 mushers compete, pulled by over 1,000 dogs.

The Comeback

Pretty Boy's racing days were not over yet. The next year, he was back in the lead when Ramy entered another big race, the Yukon Quest. The team won! Then, in 2000, Pretty Boy finally got his shot at the Iditarod.

Ramy and his team go around a curve during the 2000 Iditarod. He has since placed second at the Iditarod twice. He hopes to win the race someday.

"He was the main guy all the way to Nome," Ramy recalled. "He kept us going at an **incredible** pace."

Nine days, 9 hours, 20 minutes, and 30 seconds after the start, Ramy's team crossed the finish line in fourth place. It was his best finish yet!

"Pretty Boy did everything I asked him to—and more," said Ramy proudly.

Iditarod record holder Rick Swenson

The fastest Iditarod finish was in 2002. Rick Swenson completed the race in 8 days, 22 hours, 46 minutes, and 2 seconds.

More Than a Sport

Sled dog racing isn't just a sport. It's a chance to spend time with a great group of animals.

"Playing with the dogs is the best part," says Rachael Colbath. Many mushers would agree.

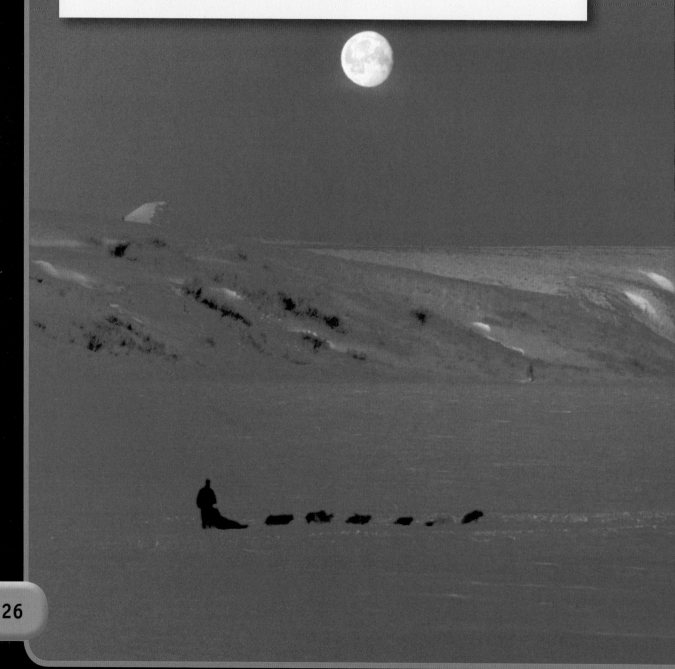

Some people worry that as land gets used up for houses and businesses, there will be less space for racing. Sled dog clubs around the country are working hard to protect their trails. In the meantime, as long as there is snow and open land, mushers and sled dogs will keep on working—and playing—together.

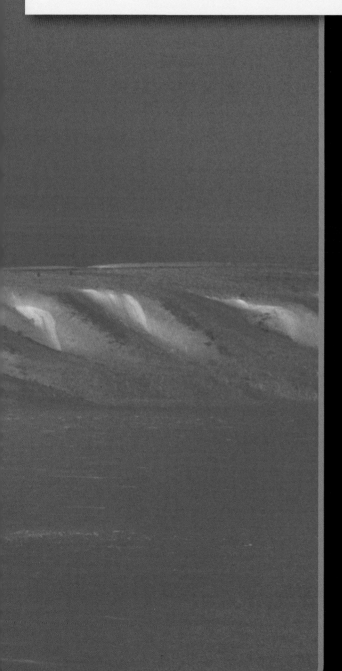

Rachael Colbath playing with Jasper, a member of her sled dog team.

There are about 6,000 mushers in the United States.

Just the Facts

- The first Iditarod race was in 1967. It was a short race, only 27 miles (43 km). Then in 1973, the race was extended to Nome. Most people consider this to be the first real Iditarod race.

- Sled dog racing is Alaska's official state sport.

- Dogsled racing is one of the few sports in which men and women compete together.

- In 1985, Libby Riddles became the first woman to win the Iditarod.

- The Red Lantern Award is given to the last-place finisher at the Iditarod. John Schultz took over a month to finish the race in 1973. His is the slowest finish on record.

- Fans visited the Iditarod Web site more than four million times during the 2004 race.

- Skijoring and bikejoring are two of the fastest-growing sled dog events. In these races, dogs pull people on skis or bikes.

- The most recent winner of the Iditarod is Robert Sorlie. He crossed the finish line on March 16, 2005.

Common Breeds: SLED DOGS

Alaskan husky

Samoyed

Alaskan malamute

Siberian husky

blizzard (BLIZ-urd) a storm with strong winds and blowing snow

bond (BOND) a strong connection with someone

commands (kuh-MANDZ) orders to do something

compete (kuhm-PEET) to try to win a contest

conditions (kuhn-DISH-uhnz) the way things are

desperate (DESS-pur-it) something that is difficult or dangerous

frostbite (FRAWST-*bite*) the freezing of fingers, toes, or other body parts

hitched (HICHD) fastened to something

incredible (in-KRED-uh-buhl) so amazing that it is hard to believe

injured (IN-jurd) harm done to your body

instinct (IN-stingkt) something a person or animal does naturally, without having to learn it

pace (PAYSS) a certain speed

purebred (PYOOR-BRED) an animal whose parents, grandparents, and other ancestors are all the same kind of animal

relay race (REE-lay RAYSS) a type of race where members of a team take turns running and passing an object from one runner to another

remote (ri-MOHT) difficult to reach

sprint (SPRINT) to run at top speed for a short distance

survive (sur-VIVE) to stay alive

tundra (TUHN-druh) an area where the ground is always frozen

wilderness (WIL-dur-niss) a place where few people live and nature grows wild

Bibliography

Cooper, Michael. *Racing Sled Dogs: An Original North American Sport.* Boston, MA: Clarion Books (1988).

O'Neill, Catherine. *Dogs on Duty.* Washington, D.C.: National Geographic Society (1988).

Salisbury, Gay, and Laney Salisbury. *The Cruelest Miles: The Heroic Story of Dogs and Men in a Race Against an Epidemic.* New York: W. W. Norton (2003).

Sled Dogs: An Alaskan Epic, a co-production of Pangolin Pictures Inc. and Thirteen/WNET New York, 1999, videocassette.

Read More

Blake, Robert J. *Togo.* New York: Philomel Books (2002).

Miller, Debbie S. *The Great Serum Race: Blazing the Iditarod Trail.* New York: Walker Books for Young Readers (2003).

Standiford, Natalie. *The True Life Story of Balto: The Bravest Dog Ever.* New York: Random House (1989).

Learn More Online

Visit these Web sites to learn more about sled dogs and sled dog racing:

www.iditarod.com

www.isdra.org

www.workingdogweb.com

Index

airplanes 5, 9, 21
Alaskan huskies 11, 12–13, 14, 29
Alaskan malamute 12, 29
Anchorage, Alaska 4, 18

Balto 6–7
Brooks, Ramy 12–13, 22–23, 24–25

Colbath, Brittany 11
Colbath, Rachael 11, 26–27
commands 14–15

dropped dogs 21

Eskimos 8

Iditarod 18, 22–23, 24–25, 28

lead dogs 16–17, 22–23, 24

mushers 4–5, 13, 14–15, 16–17, 19, 20–21, 23, 26–27

New Hampshire 10–11
Nome, Alaska 4–5, 7, 8–9, 18, 25, 28

Pretty Boy 22–23, 24–25

racing 7, 9, 10–11, 13, 14–15, 17, 18–19, 21, 23, 24–25, 26–27, 28

Samoyed 29
Siberian husky 12, 29
snowmobiles 9

teamwork 15
training 14–15, 16
transportation 8

Yukon Quest 24

About the Author

Lori Haskins has been writing and editing children's books since 1992. She lives in New York City.